ALL MY

WINGS

COLOUR
ALL MY
WINGS

A Poetry Journey

Elizabeth Ann Anderson

Moulin

Copyright © 1998 by Moulin Publishing Limited /
Elizabeth Ann Anderson

Moulin Publishing Limited
P. O. Box #560
Norval, Ontario
Canada LOP 1KO

Canadian Cataloguing in Publication Data

Anderson, Elizabeth, 1953 –
Colour all my wings: a poetry journey

ISBN 1-896867-05-7

1. Schizophrenia – Poetry.   I. Title

PS8551.N339C65   1998   C811'.54   C98-900120-2
PR9199.3A4714C65   1998

Printed and bound in Canada

1 2 3 4 5   ML   01 00 99 98

Cover and text design by Counterpunch / Linda Gustafson
Page production by Peter Ross

Dedicated to my mother and father
and my wonderful friends, who
never tire of my reciting poetry.
Love to everyone.

E.A.

Contents

Foreword

Colour All My Wings is the inspiring process of Elizabeth Anderson's life of coping with mental illness.

The Canadian Mental Health Association salutes Elizabeth's search for wholeness through mental health since our primary purpose is to promote the mental health of all people.

Mental health means striking a balance in all aspects of your life: social, physical, spiritual, economic and mental. Reaching a balance is a learning process.

The author confirms that she speaks only about her own situation. Through her chosen art form of prose and poetry, her journey reflects CMHA's belief that each person should have choices so that, when they need to, they can reach out to family, friends, formal services, self-help groups or community-based organizations.

Every day there are factors to challenge our mental health, some we can control and others which are beyond our control. Our lives may become off balance because of external or internal forces.

This book demonstrates that no matter what the reason, we can all take steps to improve our well-being and that of others.

Edward J. Pennington
General Director
Canadian Mental Health Association
National Office

Acknowledgements

I would like to acknowledge many people for always being there for me. Some very important people are all of my siblings, especially my sister Margaret, and the many great friends who never tire of my excitement at being able to have a book published. You know who you are – thank you very much. Your warm acceptance of my pleasure helped make me stay calm. I want especially to thank Mr. Ed Boyce for making this book a possibility. It was a dream that I never ever expected to have happen.

I would also like to thank George Jolly, Dr. Joanne Hoffman and Deirdre Evans of the Mount Pleasant Mental Health Care Team for their wonderful care in the many years I have been one of their clients. I'd like to thank Coast Clubhouse staff for all the wonderful support and the use of their computers to let me get the manuscript on disk. Also, I would like to thank Mary Chisholm of Milton, Ontario, for taking my rough work to Mr. Ed Boyce. I really, really appreciate that Moulin Publishing is creating this book. The last thank yous are for Rebecca Vogan and Chris Boyce for being such understanding people.

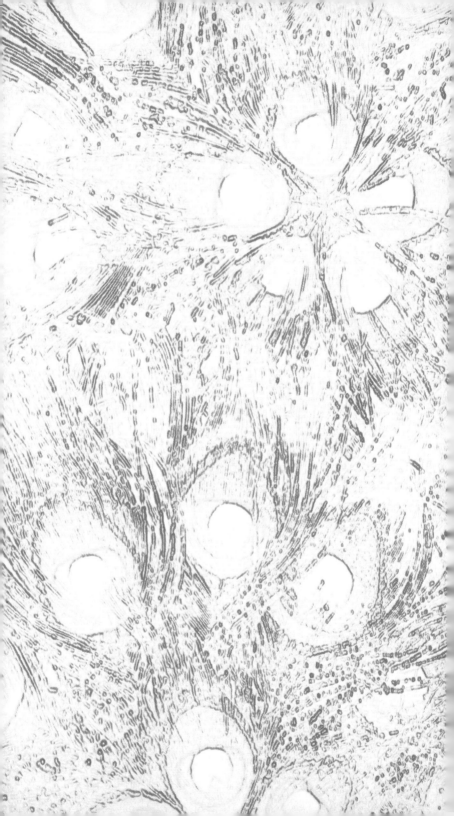

COLOUR

ALL MY

WINGS

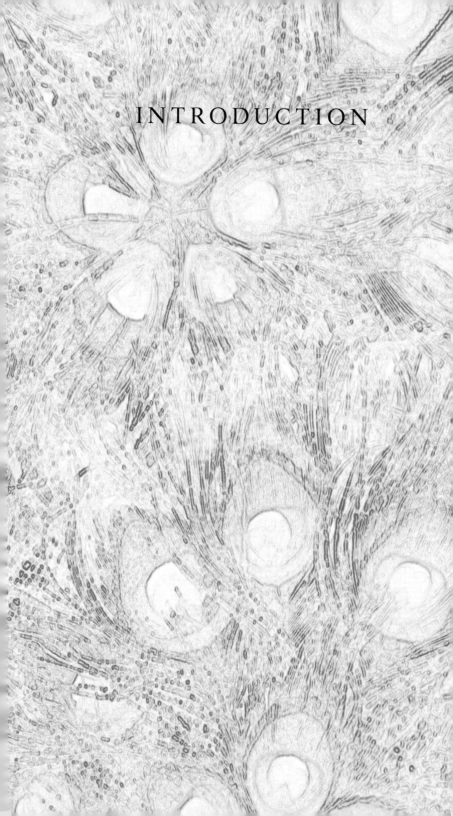

INTRODUCTION

My name is Elizabeth Ann Anderson. I was diagnosed with schizophrenia in 1979. The following is my journey.

Let me begin by telling you a little about myself.

I was born in Milton, Ontario, on November 16, 1953. I am the third child of six siblings. All of our family attended a one-room schoolhouse called Kelso School where eight grades were taught by the same teacher. I was in attendance there from Grade 1 to Grade 5, and attended Grade 6 at Campbellville Public. For Grades 7 and 8, I went to Brookville Public. I attended high school at Milton District High from 1967 to 1972 and earned a Grade 13 diploma. After this, I worked one year at Crown Life Insurance Company in Toronto while living with my uncle.

I left this job in September 1973 to attend the University of Guelph, where I obtained a general BA with a fine art specialty. During my degree, I had summer jobs in a variety of places. I worked in Banff twice and then moved on to Vancouver. I also travelled to Italy in 1975 to take two art courses, one on the Renaissance period and one on the Baroque period. I was to attend UBC in 1977 for my teacher's certificate, but I was too timid to teach at this time. Instead, I got a job making plastic jewellery from Fimo plastic, and also as a hobby learned how to weave. Then, in 1979, I had my first breakdown. I returned to Ontario to my parents, and they placed me in Hamilton Psychiatric Hospital for a period of six months, after which I again returned to the family. In November 1980, I drove across Canada to Vancouver with my boyfriend. We lived together for six months and then he returned to Ontario. I remained and my younger sister came to live with me. This was the time of my second breakdown; since then, I have had five more. (When I talk about breakdowns, I mean I was hospitalized for a period of time.)

In 1986, I went to Langara College to begin an Early Childhood Education Certificate program, which I completed in 1991. This was a very difficult certificate to obtain because I had one of my worst breakdowns in 1989. I was hospitalized for one month and attended a psychiatric day program for nine months, which basically took a whole year of my life away. At this time, I was rediagnosed with schizo-affective disorder.

I have changed anti-psychotic medication only twice, but have taken anti-depressants and lithium at different periods in my life. I found that the lithium and anti-depressants really didn't do anything except make me gain weight, which I didn't appreciate. However, I had no idea that medicines could have this effect. I require anti-psychotics to function, and since taking the new anti-psychotic Risperdal, I have been stable for almost four years without a breakdown. This is amazing, since on my previous anti-psychotic in the eighties, I could almost write my tickets for hospitalization every two to three years, even though I always followed the doctor's instructions for taking the medicine.

Now I work as an on-call substitute in different daycare sites in Vancouver and I have a position as the co-ordinator of a Community Kitchen service available at Coast Clubhouse. Coast Foundation is a mental health enhancing organization that provides people with mental health problems with a safe environment to meet and learn. It also provides subsidized housing and meals, and a Clubhouse in which to gather. I fill my need for creativity by doing craft fairs and making quilts. Of course, the most important art I am doing is writing poetry and prose about mental illness and life.

Let me tell you a little about my illness.

Staying bright and joyous is what I try to do, even when the outside world seems to be giving me messages I can't accept about my illness. I am not crazy.

I am always aware that, given enough stress, I will retreat into my fantasy world and try to recreate the whole vision from a personal perspective. I am not saying delusions and hallucinations don't have a purpose; on the contrary, I feel they keep me from destroying myself. If I didn't sometimes dream happy dreams and give myself perfect situations, the reality of my life would stop me from trying to achieve.

I have a lot of dreams and a lot of grand schemes, but each new idea gives me more certainty that with enough work on my self-development, I can help let people better understand schizo-affective disorder. I hope to do this with poetry and prose.

Someone asked me once if I had multiple personalities, and I said, "I sometimes talked like a child when I was in an acute stage of my illness, but this was a coping mechanism. It was one of my first survival impulses, but the medical attendants refused to talk to me when I did this." As I matured in my illness, I also matured in my coping skills, and I gave up this means of adapting. Instead, I created in my mind a whole scenario for every person I met, and related it in some way to myself. As you can guess, sitting on a bus, walking down a street, or even staying in a hospital became almost unachievable. Yet knowing this is how to achieve "wellness," I would remain in hospital.

Many times, I believed my food, clothing, and everyday events had an irrational significance well beyond that of ordinary necessities. Living with the delusions, and other people, made each day seem like a year, each meal seem like an incredible undertaking, and each minute crammed with events. Rest away from people was the only way I could find any reserve of energy.

With each breakdown, my creative energies peaked just before and my sleeplessness began. A lot of very good ideas came to me just before a relapse, but the act of creating brought me out of my inner world to reenter the real world. Working through my recovery by being creative (writing poetry, sewing and weaving) gave me a constructive way of releasing all my tension. These activities also gave me a lasting product to say, "This is what I did while getting well."

There are many different ways of coping, and individuals are affected by their conditions in many different ways. I speak only about my own situation.

Let me tell you a little about the poetry.

Writing poetry and prose is my chosen art form in which I express my feelings about life and how I have coped with mental illness. In the following book, I have selected poems from two diaries and restructured them in a way that I hope will allow you to share my journey. The book can be read in the order presented (by theme) or chronologically, which will give you a better sense of my daily struggles and the evolution of my coping skills. This is possible by looking at the chronological index at the back of the book and reading in the order presented. I hope you enjoy reading the book and hope that you are able to see my picture of how I am coping with my illness.

Elizabeth Ann Anderson

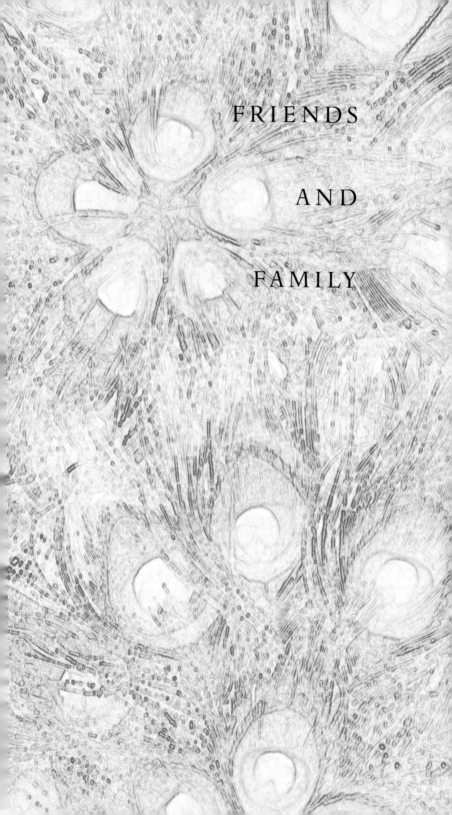

FRIENDS

AND

FAMILY

Glory to the friends who hear
The heartfelt cheer that guides me near,
To everyone who through my life
Has welcomed me despite my strife.
The struggle was the easiest kind
When no one made me feel they'd mind
If I had to lean on them
And tarry till my head would mend.
Each person in a gentle way
Gave guiding steps and words of praise.
So with each single gift of love
I choose to send my words above
Into our clear celestial sky
For others to hear and glorify.

To us, you're known as Constant Mom,
A person who was there
For every mishap of our youth
And troubles we would find.
But you're also Mom who goes to school
And Mom who volunteers and teaches
And Mom who makes the sweaters warm
And Mom who crochets afghan gifts
And Mom who listens to our woes
And Mom who understands
That life is given as a gift
To live as strong as time,
And gives us the encouragement
To make the best we can
Of every moment we receive,
To hold and share and bless,
Not just ourselves, but all our friends,
And you, Mom, who stood the test.

FRIENDS

AND FAMILY

Surrounding every friendship
Is a path of thorns and flowers,
Where I try to build a trellis
That is like a silken bower
To allow my friends to treasure
Not only what they see,
But surround them with a fragrance
That's as heavenly as Thee.
This is what I want to make
In my garden plot
So that every friend realizes
That they mean a lot.

Many are the friends I know
Who listen very carefully
To fully understand what's being said,
And gently help me reacquaint
Myself with what has happened.
They guide me in their quiet ways
To appreciate and reappraise
And recognize that every action
Both by me and my acquaintance
Cause us each to reassess
What was meant and what was said.

Appreciate the patience
That each friend shares with you,
For the guided heart of friendship
Is a ship that passes through,
And to really reap the benefit
Of passage on this boat,
It helps to always give some love
To keep the boat afloat.

Comfort & contentment,
Caring & concern,
Words of greatest pleasure,
Words of passing grief,
Words to help remember
The distant friends we greet
Even when no longer
We meet them on the street.
Sometimes we just listen,
Sometimes we explain,
But comfort & contentment
Still ofttimes will remain
After a conversation
With the person far away.
Greetings with the telephone
Are the greatest way to say
That it's still important
To remain a friend
Even if the distance
Would have made the
Friendship end.

Friends, hear me,
Family, as well:
You made it possible
For me to go into
And out of
Hospitals and care.
Without you I would have
Faltered
And become completely trapped in my mind.
You allowed me
To take my medication
And look after myself
And not cry and become completely
Defeated
By setbacks,
Which happened at both highs
And lows.
People who help me now,
Please understand: my past shaped me
And I struggle to let it go,
But the trauma of schizophrenia and mania
Leaves scars
That are hard to heal.

The Little Girl

Quietly I ask the night
To be my guide,
Gently take me down the path
To slumber's blessed journey,
Hold me in the calmest balmy sea
And shelter me from crying.
Let me see the waves of fear
Glide gently by upon the breeze
And give me solitary wisps of air
Filled with tranquillity.
And give my heart a healing balm
That I can spread with free abandon
To release the loving little girl
Who hid and remained trampled.

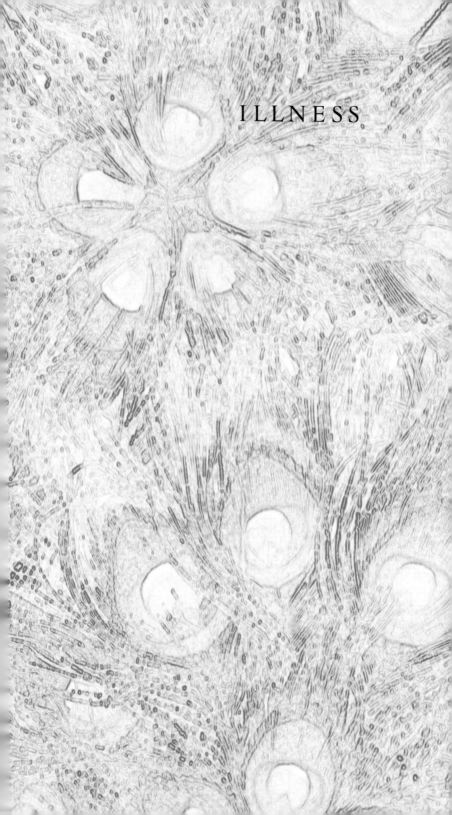

ILLNESS

I look through the window at the world,
A world of pretty pink and purple flowers
And dancing fantasies, and believe in the big, big people.

I walk through my window into the world,
A world of scornful multitudes
Forgetful of my innocence, and replace all my dreams
    with tragedy.

I was a very little girl.

The following early works show my mind jumping before diagnosis. They reveal the distortions of highs and lows I experienced while ill. All my later works were written after I changed medications to Risperdal.

Transiting the connection of real and unreal; memory
episodic dialogue.
A friend said, "Hello, where have you been?"
Reply, "In recluse."

Hiding away from society hoping to find an
accessible link with nature and mankind like
a well established garden showing love for
the soil but with only the selected species inhabiting
the area
        (aloneness maybe)
The associating with fellow man as a soother for
the social soul never seems easily accessible.
The right of speech, the ritual most demanded,
has a vocabulary of plastic thought and diverging
purpose.
Non-understanding of present, past or expectancy
of future leaves a field of void.
The shoe still walks forward with the leg,

but time bears little of the burden; mind games
with mystical reality, with absent fantasies, with
ever ongoing transit; with habitual moves from
one life cycle to another, from one land to
another; searching.

Food thoughts follow this same ceaseless journey,
passing through, pre-digested, seldom tasted, they
wither into undernourished calories of energy
stored in the superfluous coating of gathering
flesh.

The moments must be collected in chasms of time,
    accessible, retrievable, touchable (returnable?)

The soothing spell of mountain air & clear sky reaches
    into my mind, expanding the space to a border
    bounding on nothing.
The height and the joy of the voyage itself passing only
    to me in my throne.
Nature pounds forth a storm equally bright to the sun
    and moves quietly back to the blanketed flowers nes-
    tled snugly in the soft cushions of earth. The insects
    abound ranging freely, distributing life energy to the
    wind and time postulates nothing and registers only
    the beauty of breath.

The ocean is so many fathoms deep,
It holds the open secrets of the streets,
It feels the same emotion as the sky
And chanters of all religions hovering by.

The waters bashing swiftly with the tide
Hear city music playing from inside,
Trying to find some energy to last
Beyond the architectural body cast.

I wrote the the next poem while taking Stelazine, the
medication I was prescibed before changing to Risperdal.

Insight

Insight
This is mine
Struggle
I've only begun
Where it leads
How should I know
What will I do
Struggle
Freedom is a word I no longer
Expect to experience
Any time It can attack
Planning means nothing
Medication means everything
But
Hold it
That doesn't even work
I try to accept
I try to continue
I try to stay "tough" and
Accomplish

In 1994, I began taking Risperdal. The rest of the poems in this book were written after this date.

About Mental Illness   November 8, 1995

There are many times when I don't
    Fit the picture
    Stay untuned
    Show the world
    I'm unfit.
But my mind has been there!
I can understand!
Locked wards are scary!
Needles do threaten!
Pills do change
    My body!
Mental illness is a picture
    Of madness.
    That is not so.
    It's a speaking mind.
    It teaches wisdom,
    And courage,
    And determination,
    And willpower,
    And stamina,
    And love,
    Lots of love
    For everyone.

Being kept safe
From the challenges of the mind
Is the hardest thing
A family does for
Their loved ones
With schizophrenia.
Being kept safe
Seems hurtful
If it is behind locked doors.
But sometimes
The mind is so fragile,
It only wants to die
And take away the horrible thoughts
Passing through,
And end the trauma of trying
To understand.
My mind often triggered into thoughts
So bizarre and frightening
I would wish for hospitals
So I would have fewer stimuli.
Even on the scary wards with strange behaviours
People were less frightening than in the street world,
Where people try to manipulate each other.
On wards, we cared only about ourselves.

Mondrianesque November 8, 1995

I heard a young girl speak passionately
About her brother
And suicide and schizophrenia.
Both topics are dear to me.
I have the illness,
I understand the need
For freedom.
Commitment after an attempt at suicide
Might save a life
But it also might destroy a life.
The locked ward to keep me safe
Was scary.
I could easily have given up hope
And remained
Behind closed doors
For the rest of my life.
I chose to fight from inside,
Not by disobedience
Or by refusing my medication
But by passionately
Holding onto my faith in God,
By wiping the tables in the form of a cross
After each meal
For two cigarettes,
Which I didn't smoke
But gave away.

I didn't fight in any way
That was obvious.
I sanded a wooden handle
For six months without complaining,
I did needlework,
I let them cut my hair,
I even went to the dentist
(Thank God I had just seen my own dentist weeks
     before entering).
These things frightened me
Beyond belief!
But I didn't lose faith.
I had some knitting
(My family provided wool)
And I would sneak into my room
And would knit
And knit!
The lasting memory for six months
Inside a locked ward
Is a twin bedspread
Which my Mom pieced together for me
In the way I wanted to see it,
Mondrianesque.

The walls seem like a jungle.
They close around and capture.
They are not places
Where the movements are free.
There are shadows from each room,
And the staff keep moving
You towards their goal
Of passively awaiting
Each medication round,
And contemplating only
Your small role
Of being a placid person,
Never questioning an action
And always trying to please
The guarding force.
For they didn't give
Much reason
Why I had to remain captive
In this hole.

Sometimes life inside
Didn't seem so bleak.
One time at St. Vincent's
I had a very
Creative streak.
I was making coats & sweaters
And doing arts & crafts
And priding myself on
Always seeming whole.
But my mind
Was somewhat shattered
And my goals were way too much
And I was trying to achieve
A lifetime in a second
And I crashed.

We were talking about sexuality
And how it shapes our lives.
I know that it's important
To have inside,
For the message that it passes
Every day to my own soul
Is that I am a special person
Who has oftentimes been told
That sexuality is not a necessary
Force in life, you see.
But I know how it can cripple,
And I know how it can feed,
How it harms the inner spirit
When no loving friend is present,
And how comforting
The message of a lover,
Always pleasant.
Even if this secret lover
Is the spirit of the soul,
It gives the quiet message
That I'm whole.

I had to leave this lover
Many times when held inside,
And I had to crush the spirit
Of the soul.

I had to hide the feelings
That I masturbated today,
For to masturbate was forbidden
And conform the only way,
And take pills that blocked my messages
And gave a false illusion
That the pleasures of the body
Were the worst thing to display.
And I'd return to the hospital
Every time I wanted a new lover
And the pills would hold the
Rampages at bay.
But I got a new medication
That did not take love
And shutter it away.
Now I can give myself the pleasure
Of imaginary lovers
Who don't hide their inner feelings
From my soul,
And I share the secret passion
That I really am a person
Who is whole.

Guttered, frayed and torn apart
By the persistent chant
Of the untouched world
Where voices are heard only
From without
Leaving the voice within
Hollowed and echoing.
Deep enchantment fields my realm
Of quiet time,
With muse enraptured
And enthralled, with greetings
Of both night and day,
Clearly hearing what they say
No matter how absurd.
I listen and reveal the song
Of this enlightened, wonderful world.

Voice is so strong,
I want to let it sing,
I want to share the music of my mind.
I am a quiet person
In a gentle sort of way
But I share what helps me
Create my own whole.
I never walk from struggles,
I face the foe full force,
I challenge it to darken my clear road.
My path is but a journey
To a healthier person
And I gather new material
As I go.
For I travel very lightly,
I am walking by myself,
I have no companion sharing
Flight or goal.
The journey is a solitary movement
For my soul
And I waken every morning
And I whisper to my heart,
"Trust, and let go."

Understanding myself,
Allowing myself to just be,
Not trying to prove that I am strong,
Just knowing that this is so.
I've fought for education,
I've fought for health,
I've fought for acceptance.
I cannot continue to fight
For the right to be me.
I worked very hard all of the time,
Not just for someone else,
But for me,
And I feel so
Quiet
And still.
I cannot beat a loud drum
For justice.
I play a tin flute
Of a single note
To say
Justice is what I need.

Unfettered, unscathed,
Danced with the giant
And came out behaved,
Struggled with visions
So warped they could chide
That I was desperate
Only to die.
But I moved the visions
Out of the door
And I locked and bolted it,
Just as each time before.
And I continue to reach
Into my mind
To find all the glorious images
Left behind,
Waiting to be transformed
Into words of a poem
Or the wonderful artwork
For which I'll be known.

Coast Clubhouse has given me
A sanctuary,
A place where I can show my skills
But not be judged,
A place where I can meet with others
Who struggle,
A place where I can rebuild my energy
And initiative,
A place within which I can allow
The anger of frustrations
And prejudices to diminish,
A place where I can love
And open my soul to comfort
From others
And where I can give comfort to others.
We share a lifetime struggle
And by enriching another we enrich ourselves.

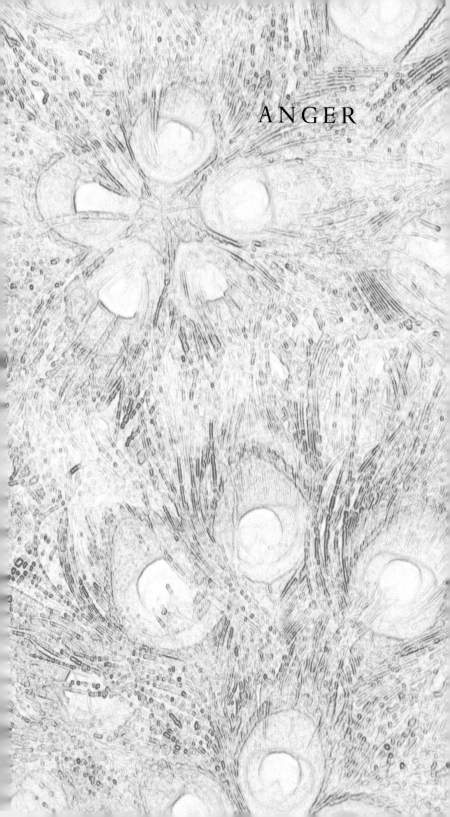

ANGER

This is what I am
Reliable
Constant
Comforting
Consoling
Encouraging
Endearing
Understanding
Considerate
All these things!
Why?
I am not that today
I am going to be hurtful
Angry
Emotional
Selfish
Defensive
And detached from
Any hard words I say

I saw a cat sitting on my window.
She meowed to be let in
But my heart was stilled.
And I wondered, would she purr?
I wondered, would she want to hide
Under my covers
Until morn?
Or would she cry more and more
And rouse the landlord from his bed
And make me
The cat at the window,
Crying to be let in,
And wondering if this plea
For sanctuary would also
Be questioned and pondered
Before the sash was opened.

There are columns found in Rome
And other places far away,
Columns in the ruins of times
And columns that record the days
Past and present, tower high,
And never let the history die.
But pillars sometimes seem so grand
That they overpower all the land
And leave the people feeling weak
Believing humble statements
Are too meek
And that only grandiose marble towers
Express the work of the artist crowd.
And all the little things we do
By creating with simple tools
And making a living from our hands,
Why aren't they also considered grand?

Daggers flash through the air.
I worry, will I be so brave
To fight this fight of fantasy?
Or will I leave
And be struck down
By the sharp reality
To say I can't imagine,
Even when I'm sure,
That my imagination
Is as clear as any mirror,
Reflecting back the image
Of the world as it is seen
And when it is distorted
Then it isn't just a dream.
It's those common daggers
That are waiting all the time
To quickly stab
And make me grab
The first shield of protection,
And leave me glad
That I can look at this with some reflection.

ANGER

Triumph over thought is so fleeting
I crave acceptance
I become submissive
Why?
Why not feel equal?
My mind is whole!
I have much to offer
My life is not useless
I've just had to counsel my soul
I AM EQUAL!

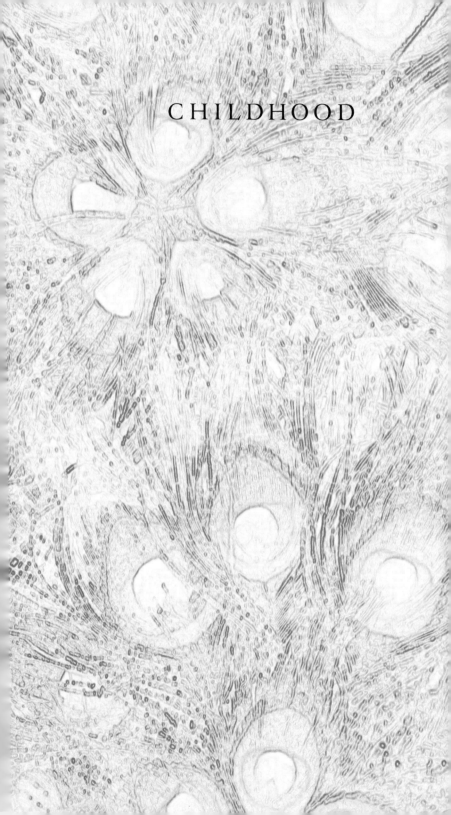

CHILDHOOD

I sow a garden in my mind,
I plant it carefully.
Each seed is spaced,
Each hill is banked,
But the crowds of nature's
Wanderlust take hold.
The twitch grass and
The pigweed,
The lamb's quarter and
The thistle,
The tame dandelion fill
The knoll.
But I hope to reap
A harvest
And I try to stem the weeds,
And I continue
With my diary
Of learning
What is me.

Mudpies with grass and leaves
Make perfect cookies
Served with tea
Of coldest, freshest water.
Children find that
They can mind a shop
Or have a party
With their friends.
Mudpies delight
As sweets of greatest fantasy
And taste delectable
As all imagery.

The dwelling that I think I want
Is like a well,
One which has a fresh spring
That replenishes the water
Each time
With a new sense of caring.
A well like the one
We had on the farm.
It served the house and the animals
And never ran dry,
It always gave
Caringly.
I reach into the well
To find my sense of worth
To find my path to the future
To find my message for today,
And I gather the water
Carefully
So as not to empty the well.

We made the forts
Of hay and boards
Within the barns and sheds.
We made the forts
Of goldenrod
At every corner post.
We made the forts
Of fallen trees
Along the mountainside.
We made the forts
Of frozen snow
And in the drifts we'd hide.
We made the forts
Throughout the year
In everything we'd find,
For forts were special places
Of the most exciting kind.
They only fit a child, you see,
No adult ever came
Within a fort to try it out,
They never played the game.
The puppies and the kittens
And the chicks, if we decided,
All played a part
Within our heart
Of space
Completely private.

CHILDHOOD

Rolling gently at first
To start the tumbling mass,
Fresh snow, new face,
Tracks of where we passed.
Clustering the balls we roll
Into a fort so tall
That we can hide behind
And throw the small snowball.
We played this game
At school and home
And ofttimes got all wet,
With mitts so sodden that they froze
And made the fingers fret:
"Can I remain and play the game
Or must I get a pair brand new?"
And play and play
Until they'd say
"We have to go in soon."

The mint grew wild
And always we would have some
When we crossed the creek.
It grew in great big
Circling patches
In the most wonderful shade of green.
We would gather
Only the upper part
Of many different plants,
So the patch would never
Die away
And the mint
Remained.

Please let me pray
For what I hoped to have,
Let me hold the pleasant picture
Of a perfect fairyland.
Let me climb up every mountain,
Let me glide down every stream,
Let me pray and dream of sunshine,
Even when the lights don't gleam.
Let me capture all the moments
Of the rollercoaster ride
That takes us down the country road
To the church where the gravestones bide.
There is much within the prayer
Of the happy joyful time,
Of the glad and rising anthems
That were sung each solemn line.
But they spread a happy message
That God's will was coming through,
And that better times were coming
And the worst was gotten through.
Each weekly blessed reminder
That we only need to pray
To find a hopeful message
On the solemnest of days.

Rushes in my mind
All filled with seeds
With red-winged blackbirds
Calling
Making spring a happy time
Walking slowly
Along the road
To the bus stop
Carefully listening
And watching
For spring
In trees, in plants, in earth
Muddy path
Frozen puddle
Frost letting go
For spring is here

Fountains with their sculpted marble
Were on every square in Rome.
They also quenched the thirst
Of tired wanderers.
Fountains of my youth
Were porcelain and pipe,
The pipe, a fresh spring spigot.
In winter this pipe would spew
A water sculpture as in Rome
Of ice and snow and droplets
All encrusted,
And we would try to break this form
So new ones were created.
But always we could have a drink
No matter what the weather.

Roadways are the paths we take
Through life.
Some are travelled single file,
Some are superhighways.
My favourite path
Was the back lane on the farm.
I could run, skip, bike or crawl.
It was well travelled half a mile
And made spring delightful
And was colourful in fall.
The path itself was two tire tracks
With hedgerows on each side,
And a middle grassy centre place
Where snakes would hide
When shy.

We had big old bicycles
With grain bags on the crossbar
For a seat.
We'd try and try
To learn to ride
And give up in defeat.
The only way I learned to ride
Was when a neighbour came
And brought a bike
The smallest size
And let me practise in the lane.
I learned so fast
And never forgot
That though they aren't the same,
The bikes of now
And the bikes of before
All have wheels, crossbars and chains.

My pen is marking moments
Of a time I welcome joyously,
A time of magic thoughts
And magic picture shows.
A time of gently wandering
About an open field
Where the grass is just a hint of space
To dance and run and play,
Where the trees are all for climbing
And the voice is sung full tilt
To the breeze that's gently blowing
Down the hill.
The cows are in the pasture,
The gates are all secure,
So I've done my work,
I've shared my joy with
Bird and breeze and land.
Now I share the magic moment
Of a time of joyful youth,
A time of growing older
But holding with life's gifts
Of memory,
Of youth.

Imaginary Life

I like to think I write a quiet sort of verse,
One that treasures past delights,
One that welcomes mirth
A verse that gives a child's desire
To touch and feel and taste
All things that come within her grasp,
And sometimes even escape
To landscapes that are make-believe
And lots of "Let's pretend,"
For children have a way, you see,
Of finding a new friend.
Even in her darkest times
A child can travel light
By reaching for the treasury
Of imaginary life.

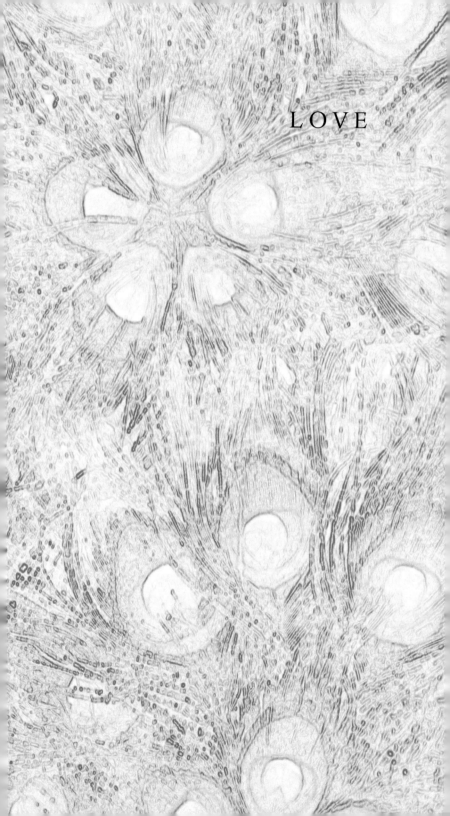

LOVE

Maybe God will hear my spirit calling to another
  And pass the message on.
Maybe God will fill my empty chambers,
  My place of dwelling which I want to share.
Maybe God will help me reach wisdom
  Enough to find the path I need to follow.
Maybe God will hear the sighs of sorrow
  For lost cherished dreams.
Maybe, God, I will get my courage
  To find a way to praise my soul,
  To give the words of worship,
  To reach for the spiritual healer
  Who welcomes all troubled girls.

Loving is a very fragile feeling

Loving is a crimson colour

Loving is a shade of grey that hurts

Loving is the inner peace of blues and pinks

Loving is the brightest star

Loving is the precious time of night we share

Loving is my thoughts for you

Love to my love

I don't write of great awakenings
Or happenings.
I write of my inner turmoil
To share my new feelings of beginnings,
My feeling I'll one day have a lover,
One day share my pleasures and pains
With someone personal,
And quiet,
And loving.
I'm lonely and awakening slowly.

I create new ideas in my mind,
I dream of making art,
I dream of a lover.
What I do is defrost my fridge,
Watch some television,
Phone friends long distance
And wander about my house
Without a purpose,
Eating,
Drinking coffee,
And wanting so badly to call him.
But he won't let me.
I know if I try,
He will reject me.
Why do I want him so?
I need to feel complete without his love.
But I dream,
And I place hope in my imagination
Which gives me promises
Of love.

I care for him within my heart.
I imagine conversations,
I idealize his qualities,
I await his words,
I watch for his notice,
I listen for his advice.
I welcome him into my being
In any way he allows,
And I console myself with
A mere fraction of the loving
Which I desire.
I care.

I want to write about happy thoughts
Because my eyes cry.
I want to think about some
Pleasure.
The time of day when I awake
And decide what I will do.
The time of night
When I write about love.
The time of hope when
I talk to others.
Share the task of living
And caring,
And comforting,
And learning,
And guiding,
And helping another pass
Time with more pleasure
And enthusiasm!
And confidence!
And dignity!
And love!

Love often doesn't come when you expect it,
Love often sneaks in and holds open a door.
Love often gains hold by dreaming
And allowing the message to flow.
Love often holds off until you are ready
To carry the burden of strife,
For love often brings many reminders
Of taking and giving in turn,
And being courageous and feisty,
Making love a conquering goal.
But love opens the doorway slowly
And enters first to the soul.
Lover, I gently remind you
That shelter will come to us both
And when it is heavenly meant
We will share our bodies and souls.

How to call a friend?
Leave a message of my love,
Fasten it with wings of hope,
Lighten it with cheer,
Gladden it with unshed tears
Of happiness abounding,
Carry it with stumbling feet
To the cherished person,
And give to him my precious love
And take away some burdens,
Lighten up the load he bears,
Give him angel choruses
Of helping friends and words of joy
To make him feel more certain.

I love my dream friend very much,
I talk to him with pleasure,
And he returns my words of love
In all his conversations.
But dream friends are so fanciful
And dream friends are so clever,
He fools me into thinking
That he really is a person.
But dream friends are just messengers
Of a kind and loyal self
That ofttimes isn't heard by me
As a voice which recommends
To think myself as a gifted self
And not just hovering coldly
Between moments of creativity
And moments of despair.

Cherish all the joy we feel,
Open-hearted warm appeal.
Cherish all the music flowing,
Gladdening echoes glowing.
Cherish all the hours spent
With each other in contentment.
Cherish all the dreams of love,
They are what we've come to have,
Moments of a happy gift
To each other gladly given,
Welcoming the warm refrain
Of a carol catching quivers,
Notes that we thought must be spent
But are still together blent.

Whisper in my heart
The love you have for me
Whisper in my ears
The words that set me free
Whisper in my soul
The trust we've come to have
Whisper to my blood
To flow with crimson love
To give my mind the touch
Of whispers from above

I cherish all the phrases
Of love you pass to me,
The kindness and the comforting,
And the guiding and the care,
The words of quiet comfort
When I'm feeling very sad
And the music of another
Which we both can share.

I feel you in my body
And I feel you in my mind,
I feel you as a spirit
That is gentle and so kind.
You listen and you ponder
Before I hear you speak,
And your guiding is so gentle
I feel I am so meek.

But you guide me and explain
That being meek is fine
And that wisdom seldom comes
To those with flashing lines.
It comes to those who treasure
Every feeling, every day,
And share their love and bonding
In a spiritual way.

LOVE

The spirit helps to carry
All the troubles that we have
And the bonding with another
Makes burdens cut in half.
But the bonding only happens
When guiding words are heard,
And to hear these quiet passages
I listen to each soft word.

I know I try to quicken
The passage of this love,
But the words I choose when speaking
Hold hope as well as speed.
I call to him in spirit
And sometimes on the phone
But I know at night and in the morning
I never am alone.

Clearly hear the music,
Softly blows the breeze,
And cylinders of glass
Resound in pleasant keys,
The gift of light refrains of song
So gently chiming out the love
Of breeze and glass with jingling strums
That float melodiously.
And quiet times when no refrain
Is heard by listeners near,
And times when glass and glass collide
So often that the music builds
A chorus of a gathering storm
And warns the people who can hear
That within each decibel of love
A storm sometimes can wait as well as dove.

Gentle harbour of light,
You hold me shyly in your beam
And give me loving words of joy
To still the dissonant roar.
When I grow dim and unsure
You brightly shine a path to follow
And bring me back from fear
To let me see more clearly.
How happy you are that I am here,
And how grateful you are
That I look for the light within my soul
And welcome the love
Held out to me
Even when I am in disharmony.

It's hard to reach the pinnacle
Of mountain peak crescendos,
The ascent may seem so visible
And steps so very simple.
But climbing high
So near the sky
Reminds the patient lover
That these ascents
Of best attempts
Can sometimes be uncertain.

Seek your heart
Play the light
And shine in the dark
Bright
Still the breath
On a winter's morn
Frosty warmth
Glowing
Puff of air and steam
Keep together
Take the dream
Into the light of day
Play
Winter enfolds you

Love, gentle spirit in my heart,
Stay in touch with all my parts.
Keep me in a kindly home,
Make me feel that I will go
To a place where there will be
Someone who will make me see
That I have been in heaven's gate,
Even though for love I wait.
I am not forever found
Staying down here on the ground,
Sometimes I just float on high
Wandering about and questioning why.
Others cannot see the choice
When you feel you've lost your voice.
Sometimes I think that if I try
I can write on stars with lullabies.

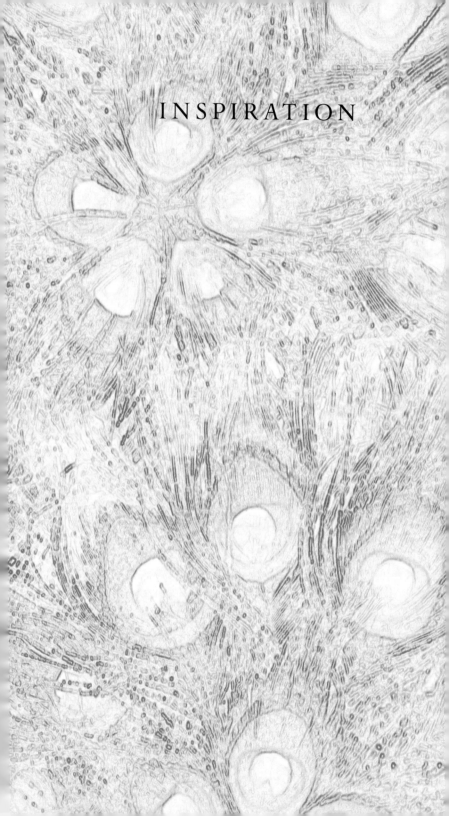

INSPIRATION

Can I see him?
Yes, I can.
But he isn't any ordinary man.
He is always giving praise
Wherever he is going
To the ones who feel rejected
Or alone.
He gives messages of progress,
He forgives the common lapses
Of the people
Who are praying for reform.
He secures the secret feelings
That there always is a saint
Within each soul.
There is someone we should treasure
In our body who is wanting to be known.
Can I see him?
Yes, I can.

Shepherd, tend your flock,
For there are many wandering.
They venture onto mountain trails
That lead to slopes of shifting shale.
Each must step with guided hoof
To keep their footing from coming loose.
Shepherd, mind your sheep,
For they are blind to waters deep
That lie in wait,
And ofttimes roam with spirits light.
Forgetting all the past travails
That were the lessons of the slopes,
They wander without cares or hopes.

Cushioning the fall
From peaks of lofty heights
I regain my marvel
At the subtle soft delights
Of sharing what we treasure
With those we care for most
And keeping all the anger
Inside so that it goes
Not into the moment
But dissipates with time
So that lofty glorious moments
Can be wonderfully sublime

Courage of Appeal   February 13, 1997

Bravely face the world
To see the magic flight
Of moving into wisdom
When I feel I have no right
To say with greatest certainty
That I am glad I share
The courage of uncertainty
That poets always bare
When they share their verses free
Even though it costs
All their hopes
And all their fears
That the meaning might be lost

I mellow into the night
To capture all disquieting muse
Of life within
Without.
Shout! that I care,
Shout! that I want,
Say only that I will remain
A raging soul,
Not shattered but revealed!
Letting the guardian angel,
Who so carefully restrained
My body from demise, retreat,
I push the spirit to
Reach the uncharted skies
Of inner harmony, and
Seek my luminosity.

Music plays a melody
That vibrates all inside
And the only way to hear it
Is to listen for the guide.
The guide's the magic person
Who dwells within the soul
And if you listen you can hear him
Conducting orchestras of old.
And also he remembers
To open up the door
So that the sounds of nature
Are appreciated more
And that the sounds within us,
Like a breath or whispered sigh,
Are not lost to the dear listener
Who remembers where and why.

Touch of tenderness,
Reach my scarred mind.
I am hiding deep inside,
Where open wounds are healing.
Wounds are felt by everyone
And need their dressings changed with care
And lots of understanding,
Freeing up the flow of healing warmth,
By seeing that each scar is
Stronger than the one before
And making ways of opening & closing,
And not tearing at the painful past
By touching scars with feather tips
Anointed in the lightest
Oils of hearing.

Gently I listen for music
That plays within my heart,
Laughing and gurgling with friendship,
Fluttering out of the dark,
Floating along with the breezes
Through windows open to say,
"Please enter and remind me
That I must work as well as play."
I'm just beginning to welcome
The words within my head
That say I am very important
And that life's to enjoy, not dread,
And that feeling I had to resist
All the happiness that passed by
Was the reason I remained so broken
And caught problems within my mind.
But now I listen for music
Of resonances that chime
And give the feeling of welcome
No matter what the time.

Child in my heart,
You're precious.
You valiantly face the world
No matter how difficult.
You tell the mind,
Be happy with what you have,
Ask only for what is presented,
Don't speak before spoken to,
And keep a cheerful disposition.
Child in my heart,
You provide the quiet reminders
That play is something I need,
And love is something I should
Accept whenever offered.
Child, I love your courage,
Child, I love your tenacity,
Child, I love your generosity,
Child, I love your happiness,
Child, I love you.

Children can make it all happen
   Pretend
Children can change their condition
   Pretend
Children can add to emotions
   Pretend
Children can play they are parents
   Pretend
Children can leap through imagination
   Pretend
Children can shelter their childhood
   Pretend
Children can heal their subconscious
   Pretend
Children can help find solutions
   Pretend
Children can harmonize with everything

Day-care Love

Each child is given a gift,
The life to live and seek.
Each child is given a harp,
Within their soul to meet.
Each child is given a start
On life by parent's words.
Each child is given a trust,
To nurture what's inside.
Each child is given a sword,
To fight the path of fear.
Each child is given a heart,
To gladden and to cheer,
To reach with open arms
For sheltered love from harms.

I am not alone.
I have my imagination
As my guide.
It is very gregarious
And playful.
It gives me worlds of pure ecstasy
And ideas to keep me happy.
Even if I am not a lover
I am a friend,
Not just to other people
But to myself.
I give loving embraces to my heart
And mind.
I give words of courage.
I give gifts of verse.
I give sighs of hope.
I give tender strokes to my body
And tell myself
I am not alone.

Thinker, why say you don't do?
Thinker, why say you don't talk?
Thinker,
    You add to everyone's day.
    You add to everyone's smile.
    You bring in ideas of warmth.
Thinker,
    You dwell in the present.
Thinker,
    You calmly explore.
Thinker,
    I welcome your words.

I can only tell little bits of the story
    At one time
I can only allow myself tiny steps
    For freedom
I have not secured my base
    On reality
I still don't know if my mind
    Can talk
I continue to think there is
    Another dimension
And my mind plays on this plane
And tells stories of my uniqueness
    And history
To you, the listener
Please understand
That I can only grow stronger
By unburdening the past
And trying to allow myself
To live in the present
And to dream about the future
Someday, I will talk to a friend
Who will be my dear listener

You are a kindred spirit
Your story is worth telling
You are my shepherd
You show me strength
You show me compassion
You show me connections
With inner harmonies
You convey with smiles
And laughter
And lovingly give praise
You share so generously
You grow bolder
And show me the caring
That you have for everyone
Don't stop the inner praise
It is so deservedly given
Peace be with you

Nakedly, I shed my skin,
I show the heart that lies within.
I venture into gallery space
And place my works to be viewed with grace
To be criticized with a caring hand,
And understand that it is a beginning, not end,
And that in all ways I continue to grow
And I'll continue to open and expose
The calling that I feel within.
I practise and perfect with time,
Never really expecting to find
The ideal I desire in my driving mind
That sees so much in everything.
And I create and recreate
With passion that has always been
The force that keeps me striving.

Taking time to gather my body
And mind and heart and soul
All in one place
Of quiet sanctuary
A place where each breath
Gives thoughts
Where each beat of the heart
Gives voice
Where the soul
Helps the spirit
Through the troubled passage
And lets my person
Move towards freedom
Where I can travel
And stay at home
At the same time
By reaching into
The sanctuary of peace
Within
For the help
For the body
I am

The sky seems so high
The sea so deep.
I wonder, will I ever
Stay inside my sleep?
I pause before I slumber
And when I first wake up,
And lead a kind of fairytale
That keeps my spirits up.
This fairyland is very real
And plays within my head
And gives me all the courage
That the world tries to knock dead.
So I let the elves play mischief
With my mind as they see fit,
For I really, really need them
To give me their benefit.

The ocean is so vast
The shore so long
The rhythm so enriching
Pass the tide
The shells of life
Are scattered
By the storm
And reach the empty beaches
When it's done
Shells vary with the ocean
They vary with the tide
But the ocean
Shares its riches
With the shore
The people pass
They lose the task
Of understanding
That each glistening shell
Tells stories
Of long ago

Dance of my mind
It twists and turns
And beats the floor
With heel and toe
And leaps and leans
And gives the music
Breathless life
In silence held
Within my heart
It holds moments
In embraces
Strongly clasped
And stumbles over
Steps misplaced
And holds together
All that's passed

Draw up a design for a quilt,
Begin a new way of creating,
Welcome the images of difference,
Seek ways to rebuild it
And make great
The pieces of fabric.
Fashion my life the same way.
Look for the strength in diversity,
Take something old and renew it,
Welcome the new friends,
Realize that more than one person
Makes living quilts in ourselves
And all are necessary
For the whole.

A chapter of life is flowing,
Bringing the tide to the shore,
Starting a path of renewal,
Giving meaning to my soul.
Making me think I'm important
Not just to the people I meet,
But saying I'll make sure I'm safe,
And not feeling I must do all
Without retreat.
I am just as important
As any task I attempt
And I'm going to keep thinking safety
And keep my health as my goal,
For I am not just a survivor
But a messenger too.
Take care of the soul
And God will take care of you.

Caring for people I admire
Makes caring for myself easier,
And caring for myself
Is the best way to help me
Help another.
I care for my spirit with gentle caresses
And warming words of comfort.
I add calming phrases to the
Discordant vibrations of my life.
And I imagine conversations
With my mentor,
Who calmly tells me to explore
The possibility in friendship
And consider that
My wishes are being heard.

Colour all my wings,
Not just the ones you see,
Colour all the threads of gauze
Floating gracefully.
Colour all the hidden curves
Close beside my breast,
Add colour to the underside
For that is what I show,
Not the fancy outer shell
Of a monarch's brightest flame,
But the mothlike harmony
Where blending in restrains
The glorious palette of my brush
And gives me humbling fame.

Chronological Index

INDEX

Alphabetical Index

This book was set in Dante. Although based on the
    Aldine Oldstyle romans of the 1490's, it was designed in
    1947–54 by the renowned scholar and printer, Giovanni
    Mardersteig, of the Officina Bodoni in Verona, Italy.
    It was cut in 1954 by Charles Malin.
The sans serif used is Syntax, also based on Renaissance
    forms, designed by Hans Eduard Meier and released
    by the Stempel foundry in 1969.
Printing was done by Metrolitho Inc. (Transcontinental
    Printing Inc.), on 70 pound Unipaque.